*Little things
that shine
as big
as the sky.*

— JOHN HAY

Childhood Prayers – Signs of Learning®

— *For Alice B. B., her family and friends* —

Registered Title: Murray David Harwich III

Text ©2020 Mary Belle Harwich

Illustrations ©2020 Barbour Lee

ALL RIGHTS RESERVED

Printed in the United States

Published Frankfort, KY

Book Designs by Marjorie Snelson Design

ISBN 978-0-9888973-0-4

Library of Congress Control Number: 2020906548

To order printed books: www.amazon.com

Childhood Prayers

Signs of Learning®

Prayer Selections by Mary Belle Harwich

Pictures by Barbour Lee

For _____

_____

From _____

_____

Barbour Lee

I

Thank you for the
world so sweet.

Thank you for the
food we eat.

Thank you for the
birds that sing,

Thank you, Lord, for
everything

II

I see the moon,

the moon sees me,

Down through the leaves
of the old oak tree.

God bless the moon, and

God bless me.

And God bless the ones I love.

III

Now run along home,

Jump into bed

Say your prayers
and cover your head.

The very same thing I say unto you
You dream of me,

and I'll dream of you.

IV

Day is done,

Gone the sun,

From the lakes,

From the hills,

From the sky.

All is well,

Safely rest,

God is nigh.

V

Now I lay me down to sleep.

I pray the Lord my soul to keep.

His love to guide me through the night,

And keep me safe 'til morning light.

And in the morning when I wake,

Show me the path of love to take.

And thank you for this busy day —

A day to work,

A day to play.

VI

The Lord is my shepherd.

Match the number in the corner – ▢ – to the number of the poem *and find the word!*

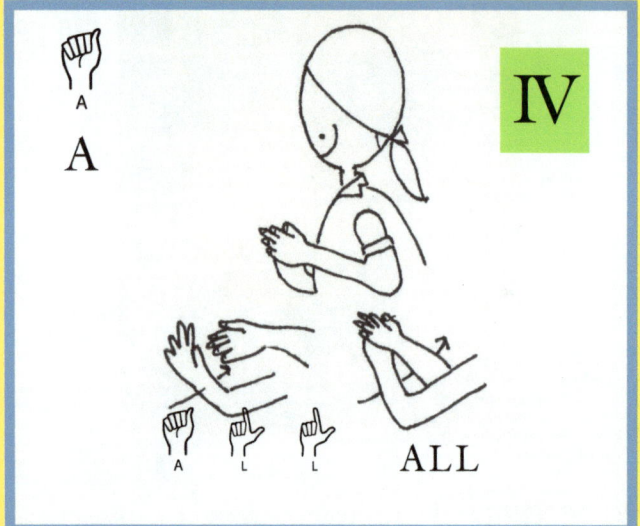

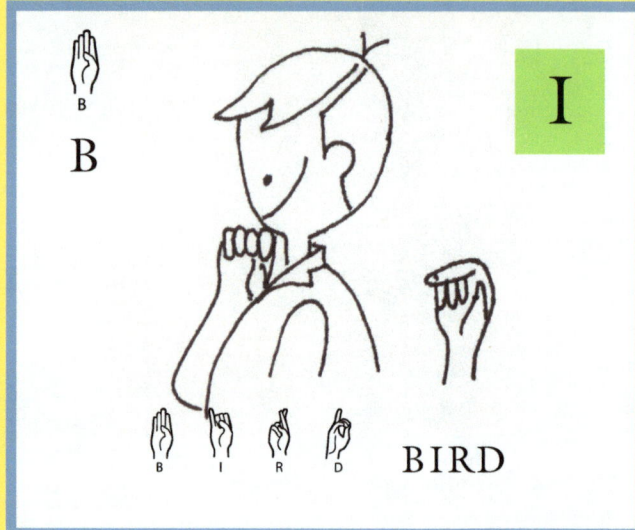

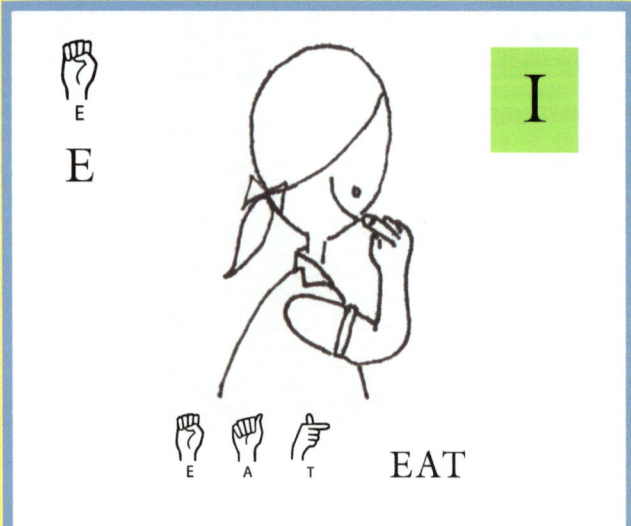

I = 1   II = 2   III = 3   IV = 4   V = 5

G — GOD — II	H — HOME — III
I — I — II	J — JUMP — III
K — KEEP — II	L — LOVE — IV

Match the number in the corner – ☐ – to the number of the poem
and find the word!

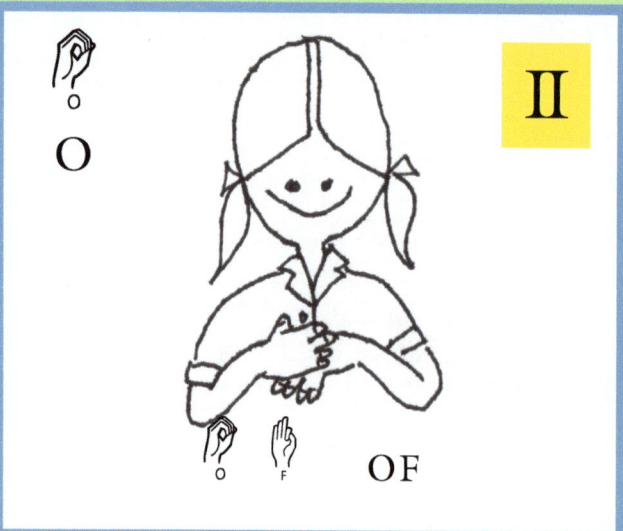

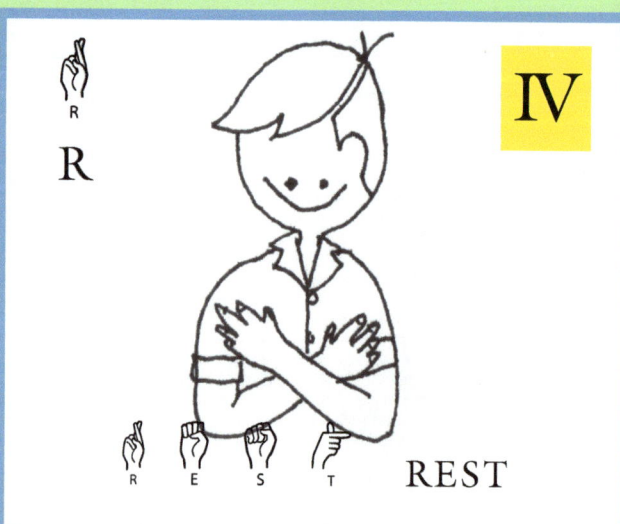

I = 1   II = 2   III = 3   IV = 4   V = 5

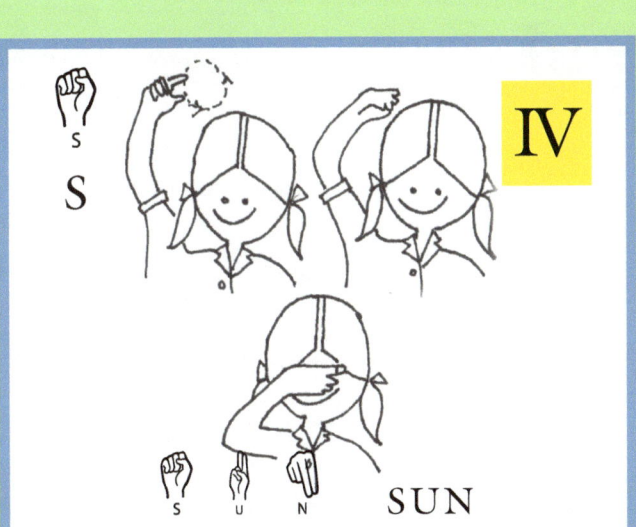
S — SUN — IV

T — TREE — II

U — UNTO — III

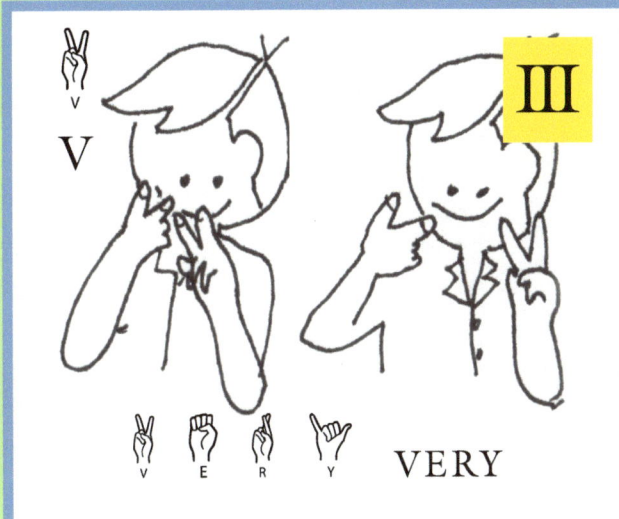
V — VERY — III

W — WORK — V

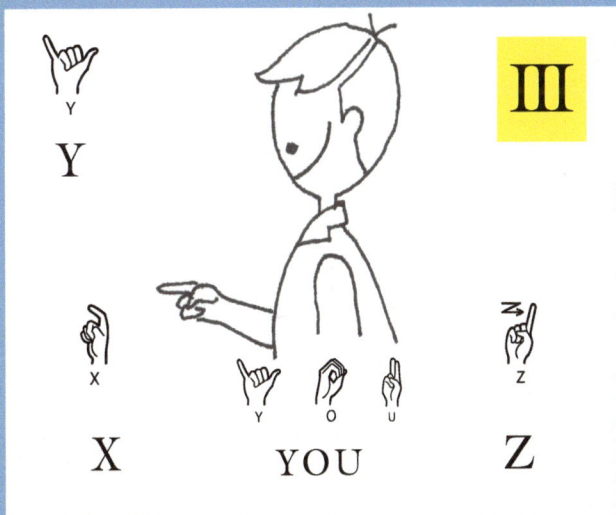
X — YOU — Z — III

House

Flowers

Kittens and Cat